MW00915094

HIRAM R. DIAZ III

The Gospel Comes With A House Key: A Critical Review

Unveiling Its Postmodern Philosophy & Feminist Theology

SCRIPTURALIST
PUBLICATIONS

First published by Scripturalist Publications 2020

Copyright © 2020 by Hiram R. Diaz III

All rights reserved. No part of this publication may be reproduced, stored or transmitted in any form or by any means, electronic, mechanical, photocopying, recording, scanning, or otherwise without written permission from the publisher. It is illegal to copy this book, post it to a website, or distribute it by any other means without permission.

Hiram R. Diaz III asserts the moral right to be identified as the author of this work.

First edition

This book was professionally typeset on Reedsy. Find out more at reedsy.com

Contents

1

Introduction

In her article for Christianity Today titled *My Train Wreck Conversion*, Dr. Rosaria Butterfield reflects on her past as "a professor of English and women's studies, on the track to becoming a tenured radical."[1] She describes herself as one who "cared about morality, justice, and compassion,"[2] and being "fervent for the worldviews of Freud, Hegel, Marx, and Darwin...strove to stand with the disempowered."[3] This description of herself is important because it portrays her as an opponent of the postmodernism and feminism from which she was converted.[4] However, a critical analysis of Butterfield's latest book *The Gospel Comes With a House Key: Practicing Radically Ordinary Hospitality in Our Post-Christian World* reveals that this is not the case.

Because the book is a series of non-academic reflective essays, it is easy to miss Butterfield's dependence on and employment of postmodern and feminist concepts, a reality which has seemingly left many readers with the impression that her understanding of hospitality is derived from Scripture. Therefore, it is the aim of this essay to bring Butterfield's philosophical roots and fruit into full view, revealing how they inform her doctrine of hospitality, how they subtly subvert Christian orthodoxy, and why Christians should steer clear of her writings.[5]

This will be accomplished by first briefly reviewing Jacques Derrida's concept of *true hospitality/pure hospitality*, and demonstrating how it stands in contradiction to the Christian concept of hospitality. From this initial step, we will move on to compare Butterfield's concept of hospitality to that of Derrida, and highlight some ways in which Butterfield's doctrine deviates from the Christian doctrine of hospitality. Following this, we will draw attention to four postmodern concepts which are embedded in *The Gospel Comes With a House Key*'s essays. These concepts are –

1. *Labeling/Categorizing as "Violence" Against the Other*
   2. *The Other/Stranger as Absolute Other/God*
   3. *Fluid Subjectivities*
   4. *The Feminist-Theological Ethic of Hospitality*

We will conclude by giving a brief summary of the postmodern philosophical roots of Butterfield's doctrine of hospitality, recapitulating how those roots subvert Christian orthodoxy, and admonishing Christians to steer clear of her writings.

2

Hospitality is Deconstruction

Derrida's Notion of Hospitality

From the onset, it should be noted that "hospitality" is a concept that has been widely discussed in postmodernist literature. One of the more influential postmodernist philosophers to discuss the concept is the father of deconstruction, Jacques Derrida. The concept is inextricable from his entire corpus of writings, and it is characterized by Derrida as a concrete instance of deconstruction. As he puts it –

> Hospitality is the deconstruction of the at-home; deconstruction is hospitality to the other.[6]

This is because, according to Derrida, pure hospitality entails no economy of exchange between guest and host, and it does not set fixed boundaries on the identities of guest and host.

Mark W. Westmoreland expounds on this, writing –

The master of the home, the host, must welcome in a foreigner, a stranger, a guest, without any qualifications, including having never been given an invitation. […] In order to offer unconditional hospitality, the master must not allow for any debt or exchange to take place within the home. No invitation, or any other condition, can ever be a part of absolute hospitality. Hospitality, as absolute, is bound by no laws or limitations. The host freely shares her home with the new arrival without asking questions. She neither asks for the arrival's name, nor does she seek any pact with the guest. Such a pact would instigate the placing of the guest under the law. The law of absolute hospitality does not involve an invitation, nor does it involve an interrogation of the guest upon entering.[7]

As Jason Foster explains,

Pure hospitality for Derrida means the complete foregoing of all judging, analyzing, and classifying other people that he believes are hallmarks of "actual hospitality". Derrida believes we must forego all "violence" that tries to conform anyone into our own image through the setting of behavioral conditions on our extension of hospitality, or by slotting people into our own pre-determined categories. *An attitude of pure hospitality embraces an utter unconditionality and readiness to give everything we have for any and every other person.* Put simply, to place limits or conditions on our extension and practice of hospitality is to commit an act of

4

violence through exclusion and coercive conformity.[8]

Derrida's concept of *pure hospitality* is recognized by him to be an ideal that will ever elude human interactions due to our finitude, resulting as it inevitably does in an aporia.[9] Westmoreland writes –

> Before the arrival of the guest, the master, or host, of the house was in control. [...] It would be assumed that the host secures the house in order to "keep the outside out" and holds authority over those who may enter the home as guests. Derrida writes that hospitality cannot be "without sovereignty of oneself over one's home, but since there is also no hospitality without finitude, sovereignty can only be exercised by filtering...and doing violence." Limits and conditions are set in place to secure the [host] as master of the house. As such, these conditions betray the law of absolute hospitality.[10]

Nevertheless, as Richard Kearney and Kascha Semonovitch rightly note, "it is difficult to not read Derrida as suggesting that absolute hospitality might well serve as a regulatory ideal, unachievable but desirable."[11] For instance, Derrida writes –

> Let us say yes to who or what turns up, before any determination, before any anticipation, before any identification, whether or not it has to do with a foreigner, an immigrant, an invited guest, or an unexpected visitor, whether or not the new arrival is the citizen of another country, a human, animal,

or divine creature, a living or dead thing, male or female.[12]

The ideal form of hospitality toward which actual hospitality should strive, then, is one which is free of all binary oppositions.[13]

3

Derridean Hospitality Vs. Christian Hospitality

A True Binary Opposition

According to Derrida *pure hospitality*, i.e. the ideal form of hospitality, results in

> ...an antinomy, an insoluble antinomy, a non-dialectizable antinomy between, on the one hand, The law of unlimited hospitality (to give the new arrival all of one's home and oneself, to give him or her one's own, our own, without asking a name, or compensation, or the fulfilment of even the smallest condition), and on the other hand, the laws (in the plural), those rights and duties that are always conditioned and conditional, as they are defined by the Greco-Roman tradition and even the Judeo-Christian one...[14]

In light of these supposed "insoluble antinomies," between "pure" hospitality and conditional hospitality, it becomes clear that Derrida's doctrine of hospitality stands in contradiction to the Christian doctrine of hospitality. For as Foster correctly notes, Derrida's failure to

> ...take seriously the current eschatological situation of boundaries that God has established during this period of redemptive history...necessitates a rather bizarre interpretation of Genesis and Revelation. In Derrida's approach, the hospitable reception of the serpent by Adam and Eve in Genesis 3 must be viewed as an act of great hospitality that should be applauded, while the prohibition to eat from the tree of the knowledge of good and evil in Genesis 2 must now be seen as a great act of inhospitality by God that violently insisted on Adam and Eve's conformity. On the other hand, the violent destruction of the serpent by God in Revelation 20 that is the triumphal source of the Christian's eschatological hope must now be viewed as inhospitably brutal and should be condemned. When Satan stands poised to eat the newborn child of promise in Revelation 12:4, the snatching up of the child by God and taking him to heaven as an act of divine protection instead must now be seen as an act of inhospitable deprivation toward Satan.[15]

These conclusions not only "contradict[...] the Johannine witness completely,"[16] but the whole of God's revelation. Derridean pure hospitality inverts the Christian faith in its entirety.

This is, largely, due to its rejection of transcendence in general, and, in particular, its rejection of a transcendent rule or set of rules that universally and absolutely determines the limits of all being and thinking and action.

As Westmoreland explains, Christian hospitality is conditional. He writes –

> Conditional hospitality concerns itself with rights, duties, obligations, etc. It has a lineage tracing back to the GrecoRoman world, through the Judeo-Christian tradition...It has been regulated.
>
> [...]
>
> ...hospitality has been reciprocal, engaged in an economy of exchange, even an economy of violence...In other words, an exchange takes place between the host and the guest. In offering hospitality, in welcoming the other, the host imposes certain conditions upon the guest. First, the host questions and identifies the foreigner. "What is your name? Where are you from? What do you want? Yes, you may stay here a few nights." Secondly, the host sets restrictions. "As my guest, you must agree to act within the limitations I establish. Just don't eat all my food or make a mess."[17]

M.T. LaFosse, summarizing Arterbury's findings, further elaborates on the conditional nature of Christian hospitality. LaFosse –

Far from being synonymous with "table fellowship," hospitality involved a series of dynamic elements, with some variation over time and culture. In broad terms, hospitality involved the host or traveling guest formally approaching the other. The host led the guest (who may be a god or angel in disguise) home, and offered provisions (water to wash, a meal, lodging) and protection. A relationship of reciprocity and permanence was often forged.[18]

Foster's account of the reciprocal exchange which took place between guest and host in Christian hospitality, is helpful here. Foster explains that

...the ultimate reception of a stranger occurred in three stages. First, the stranger was tested in order to determine if they would subscribe to the norms of the community and not threaten its purity. Second, the stranger takes on the role of a guest of the host. The roles of guest and host were culturally well defined, with requirements concerning duties and manners being placed on both, including reciprocity. Third, the stranger leaves the company of his host either as a friend or an enemy.[19]

The Christian doctrine and practice of hospitality, thus, stands in marked contrast to "the contemporary Western idea of hospitality as casual and mostly non-binding,"[20] a view which has the postmodern ideal of "pure hospitality" as its goal, and which seems to be, at least to a significant degree, shared by Rosaria Butterfield in her book *The Gospel Comes with a House*

Key.

4

Butterfield's Postmodern Roots

1. Labeling/Categorizing as "Violence" Against the Other

The Gospel Comes With a House Key (hereafter, TGH) opens with the claim that

> ...those who [practice radical ordinary hospitality] see strangers as neighbors and neighbors as family of God. They recoil at reducing a person to a category or a label. They know they are like meth addicts and sex-trade workers. They take their own sin seriously—including the sin of selfishness and pride.[21]

Rather than merely preaching at lost people, hospitality involves personal *investment* in strangers with the hope of "rendering [them] neighbors and neighbors family of God."[22] Investment of this kind stands in contradiction to what she calls "sneaky evangelistic raids into [unbelievers'] sinful lives,"[23] raids which seemingly treat one's neighbor as "a caricature of an alien world-view."[24] "Radically ordinary hospitality," she states, "values the time it takes to *invest in relationships*, to *build bridges*, to *repent of sins of the past*, to *reconcile*."[25] Butterfield expands on this, writing –

> *Engaging in radically ordinary hospitality means we provide the time necessary to* build strong relationships with people who think differently than we do *as well as build strong relationships from within the family of God. It means we know that only hypocrites and cowards let their words be stronger than their relationships,* making sneaky raids into culture on social media or behaving like moralizing social prigs in the neighborhood.[26]

For Butterfield, true hospitality, which involves becoming personally invested in those to whom we evangelize, stands in contradiction to "counterfeit hospitality" which "separates host and guest in ways that *allow no blending* of the two roles."[27] As she explains, "counterfeit hospitality creates *false divisions* and *false binaries*: noble givers or needy receivers. Or hired givers and privileged receivers.[28]

Like Derrida, Butterfield believes that central to hospitality is the rejection of labels, categories, and "false" binary oppositions which will limit or constrain our practice of hospitality toward our guests. And like Derrida, Butterfield views such limiting/-constraining (based on reductive categorization/labeling) as an act of *violence.* Butterfield writes –

> Our lack of genuine hospitality to our neighbors—all
> of them, including neighbors in the LGBTQ com-
> munity—explains why counterfeit hospitality seems
> attractive. Our lack of Christian hospitality is a
> violent form of neglect for their souls.[29]

This "genuine hospitality," it should be remembered, is one in which guests are not "reduced" to categories or labels, in which our hospitality is not constrained or limited by our consideration of the place guests occupy in a particular category.

By engaging in labeling, categorizing, and determining our behavior on the basis of labeling and categorizing, we are, according to Butterfield, committing an act of violence. In a word, she believes that "exclusion of people for arbitrary reasons—not church discipline–related ones (an important exception I discuss in chapter 6)—is *violent* and *hostile*."[30] Butterfield is not merely talking about the exclusion of Christians, however, but includes under the category of hospitality the act of "[making] room for a family displaced by a flood *or a worldwide refugee crisis.*"[31] She elaborates on this elsewhere, writing –

> It is deadly to ignore biblical teaching about serving
> the stranger—deadly to the people who desperately
> need help and deadly to anyone who claims Christ
> as King. Membership in the kingdom of God is
> intimately linked to the practice of hospitality in this
> life. Hospitality is the ground zero of the Christian
> life, biblically speaking. A more crucial question for

the Bible-believing Christian is this: Is it safe to fail to get involved?

Jesus says, "I was hungry and you gave me food, I was thirsty and you gave me drink, I was a stranger and you welcomed me, I was naked and you clothed me, I was sick and you visited me, I was in prison and you came to me" (Matt. 25:35–36). When we feel entitled to God's grace, either because of our family history or our decision making, we can never get to the core sentiment behind Jesus's words. What would it take to see Jesus as he portrays himself here? To see ourselves? Is our lack of care for the refugee and the stranger an innocent lack of opportunity, or is it a form of willful violence?[32]

This effectively identifies any non-ecclesial act of disciplinary exclusion, seemingly toward *any* stranger, as an act of *violence*. For Butterfield, "Christian hospitality [i.e. true hospitality, as opposed to counterfeit hospitality] *violates* the usual *boundary maintenance* enacted by table fellowship."[33]

Readers unfamiliar with postmodernist literature may not be aware of the fact that within postmodern thought the term *violence,* as Iddo Landau explains, "is used by many postmodernists to refer to a wide array of phenomena."[34] Included within this "wide array of phenomena," "Derrida argues that there is…the violence of *the difference*, of *classification*, and of *the system of appellation* [i.e. taxonomization]."[35] For Derrida, differentiation, classification, and taxonomization are acts of *violence*. Derrida's thinking in this regard is shared by virtually all other postmodernists. Postmodernists, James R. Dawes writes, believe that –

> The act of naming is a matter of forcibly imposing a sign upon a person or object with which it has only the most arbitrary of relationships. Names produce an Other, establish hierarchies, enable surveillance, and institute violent binaries: Naming is a strategy that one deploys in power relations. The violence cuts through at all levels, from the practically political ("They are savages," "You are queer") to the ontological (one critic writes of "the irreducibility of violence in any mark").[36]

For postmodernists and Butterfield, hospitality deconstructs "violent" labels, categories, false binaries, and divisions, by "violat[ing] the usual boundary maintenance enacted by table fellowship."[37]

2. The Other/Stranger as Absolute Other/God

Butterfield's idea of hospitality includes the belief that we can "see Jesus in those in need."[38] This broad characterization of those in whom we can see Christ is, in part, based on her interpretation of Matt 25:35-36. Seeing Jesus in others is "risky," she argues, warning that, on the one hand, "when we fail to see Jesus in *others*, we cheapen the power of the image of God to shine over the darkness of the world,"[39] and, on the other hand, that "when we always see him in *others*, we fail to discern that we live in a fallen world, one in which Satan knows where we live."[40] While Butterfield differentiates between seeing

Jesus and Satan in the stranger/guest, she nevertheless says that we can see Jesus in *others*, which is to say those *in need*, indiscriminately considered. Butterfield does not differentiate between believers who are in need and unregenerate persons who are in need. Rather, for Butterfield, Jesus can be seen in the other/one in need/guest/stranger, indiscriminately considered.

Scripture, however, clearly teaches that *only* those who are being sanctified by the Spirit of God are those in whom we can "see Jesus." This is because the children of God, alone, are being made in the image and likeness of the Son. Paul writes –

> If then you have been raised with Christ, seek the things that are above, where Christ is, seated at the right hand of God. Set your minds on things that are above, not on things that are on earth. For you have died, and your life is hidden with Christ in God. When Christ who is your life appears, then you also will appear with him in glory.

> Put to death therefore what is earthly in you: sexual immorality, impurity, passion, evil desire, and covetousness, which is idolatry. On account of these the wrath of God is coming. In these you too once walked, when you were living in them. But now you must put them all away: anger, wrath, malice, slander, and obscene talk from your mouth. Do not lie to one another, seeing that you have put off the old self with its practices and have put on the new self, which is being renewed in knowledge after the image of its creator. Here there is not Greek and Jew, circumcised

and uncircumcised, barbarian, Scythian, slave, free;
but Christ is all, and in all.[41]

Paul's words here are very clear. It is *solely* those who have
been raised with Christ who can put on the new man which is
being renewed according to the image of the Son. The image
of Jesus as that into which Christians *are being* formed via the
Holy Spirit's work of sanctification.[42] According to Scripture,
the image of the Son of God is the goal of sanctification, which
will only be complete upon our glorification. As the apostle
elsewhere writes –

> ...we know that for those who love God all things
> work together for good, for those who are called ac-
> cording to his purpose. For those whom he foreknew
> he also predestined to be conformed to the image of
> his Son, in order that he might be the firstborn among
> many brothers. And those whom he predestined he
> also called, and those whom he called he also justified,
> and those whom he justified he also glorified.[43]

Paul does not identify *every* person in need as potentially one in
whom we can "see Jesus." Rather, Paul explicitly teaches us that
it is only the elect of God in whom we may see the image and
likeness of Christ. The apostle clearly explains that the image
of Jesus consists in holiness and righteousness, and it stands in
contradiction to the "old self" which bears the moral/spiritual
image of Satan and all who are in him.[44]

Butterfield, therefore, is correct to note that we are all the imago
dei, and that as Christians we ought to recognize this and treat

others accordingly with due respect and dignity.[45] However, her belief that we can see *Jesus* in others – including the lost – is wrong. It is a belief that has more in common with the postmodern ethical theorizing of French Jewish philosopher Emmanuel Levinas, a seminal influence on Jacques Derrida's own ethical and religious theorizing. Manuel Cruz explains that for Levinas,

> In the face of the Other, one is confronted with a dialectical oscillation between the revelation of its infinite transcendence and its finitude: "This gaze that supplicates and demands, that can supplicate only because it demands, deprived of everything because entitled to everything . . . To recognize the Other is to recognize a hunger. To recognize the Other is to give. But it is to give to the master, to the lord, to him whom one approaches as "You" in a dimension of height" (Levinas [1961] 1969). Let us note the paradox: recognizing the other as vulnerable and deprived, as finite, depends on first recognizing the eminence and excess of its lordship as the infinite. The ethical significance of finitude depends on the prior significance of the infinite. There is a provocative intimation that the person I encounter on the street—subject to hunger, poverty, and murder—arrays itself with all the transcendent stature of a god, in essence signifying this vulnerable human in some way divine.[46]

Every person, Levinas believes, is one through whom we have an ethical encounter with a third person beyond – namely,

God. This is pertinent to note because although Levinas primarily reflects upon and discusses writings within the Continental philosophical tradition, as well as various Old Testament passages, he sometimes sets his attention on the New Testament.

Of particular significance here is Levinas' interest in Matthew 25:31-46, a pericope of Scripture which he claims exemplifies his ethical theory. As Kajornpat Tangyin explains,

> When Levinas mentions the teaching in…Matthew 25, he reminds us [that] the way we treat the other is the way we treat God. The infinite [i.e. God] is revealed through the other…Ethical relation, for him, begins with the response to the other's material needs. To feed the hungry, clothe the naked, give drink to the thirsty, give shelter to the shelterless, are my responsibilities.[47]

Levinas believes this particular section of the New Testament reflects his own ethical belief that every individual, regardless of his relation to God religiously/spiritually, shows God to us. He explains –

> The teaching in [the Gospels], and the representation of human beings in them, appeared always familiar to me. As a result, I was led to Matthew 25, where the people are astonished to hear that they have abandoned and persecuted God. They eventually find out that while they were sending the poor away, they were actually sending God himself away.[48]

On Levinas' view, Jesus is teaching that when the poor – indiscriminately considered – are "sent away" and "persecuted" it is actually Christ who is being sent away and persecuted.[49] As he explains elsewhere, in Matthew 25:31-46 "the relation to God is presented…as a relation to *another* [human] *person*."[50]

What is absent from Levinas' treatment of the passage, as well as from Butterfield's use of the passage, is the Lord Jesus' explicit identification of the recipients of mercy as "brothers." Christ unambiguously declares – 'Truly, I say to you, as you did it to one of the least of these *my brothers*, you did it to me.'[51] These "brothers," let us remember, are not the poor indiscriminately considered but *only* Christians. We know this because Christ states that "whoever does the will of [his] Father in heaven is [his] *brother*,"[52] including not only the eleven disciples[53] but every Christian,

> For he who sanctifies and those who are sanctified all have one source. That is why [Christ] is not ashamed to call them brothers, saying,
>
> "I will tell of your name to my brothers;
>   in the midst of the congregation I will sing your praise."[54]

The brothers of Christ, "the least of these," then, are those toward whom the Holy Spirit commands us to show hospitality. New Testament passages dealing with hospitality, moreover, have to do with Christian behavior toward other brothers.

> Contribute to the needs of the saints and seek to show

hospitality.[55]

Let a widow be enrolled if she is not less than sixty years of age, having been the wife of one husband, and having a reputation for good works: if she has brought up children, has shown hospitality, has washed the feet of the saints, [cf. John 13:12-20] has cared for the afflicted, and has devoted herself to every good work.[56]

Let brotherly love continue. Do not neglect to show hospitality to strangers, for thereby some have entertained angels unawares. Remember those who are in prison, as though in prison with them, and those who are mistreated, since you also are in the body.[57]

The end of all things is at hand; therefore be self-controlled and sober-minded for the sake of your prayers. Above all, keep loving one another [within the body of Christ] earnestly, since love covers a multitude of sins. Show hospitality to one another [within the body of Christ] without grumbling. As each has received a gift, use it to serve one another, as good stewards of God's varied grace…[58]

Contrary to the kind of thinking espoused by Levinas and Butterfield, it is *only* in *Christians* who are strangers, imprisoned, hungry, thirsty, and naked that we see Christ.

3. Fluid Subjectivities

We began our exploration of Butterfield's postmodern ideas with a comparison of her concept of hospitality to Derrida's concept of pure hospitality. We then moved on to consider the similarities between Butterfield's belief that Jesus can potentially be seen in any other human being – regenerate or un-regenerate – and Levinas' belief that every other stranger/needy human is, in fact, Christ, i.e. God, himself, specifically drawing attention to the similarities between Butterfield and Levinas' misinterpretation of Matt 25:31-46. We now will focus our review on Butterfield's implied concept of *fluid subjectivity*. Given that *TGH* is not dealing primarily with subjectivity, we will draw on some of her earlier work to demonstrate *TGH*'s implicit concept of *fluid subjectivity*.

First, however, we must disambiguate the term *subjectivity*. The popular use of the word "subjectivity" is defined as "the quality, state, or nature of being subjective,"[59] wherein the term subjective is to be understood as signifying something that is, or is capable of being or having been, "modified or affected by personal views, experience, or background."[60] The term *subjectivity* within academic contexts, however, is a technical term whose meaning is only partly resonant with popular use. As Marina F. Bykova explains –

> Originally, [subjectivity] was used to designate all that refers to a subject's psychological-physical integrity represented by its mind, which determines the unique mentality, psychological state, and reactions of the subject. In this use, subjectivity meant the conscious-

ness of one's real self (self-consciousness), where the real self is what unites the disparate elements.[61]

Central to the modernist conception of subjectivity is the assumption of integrity, unity, and autonomy. With the advent of postmodernism, however, this changed. Postmodern philosophers deconstructed the concepts of unity, integrity, and autonomy, and consequently proclaimed "the death of the subject,"[62] which in turn "necessitated the development of new approaches to the classical and modern concepts of subject and subjectivity."[63] Subjects are fluid, not fixed; identities have *permeable* boundaries, not uncrossable borders.

In *TGH*, the idea of fluid subjectivity appears as an assumed reality. For instance, Butterfield makes the claim that "in radically ordinary hospitality, *host and guest are interchangeable*,"[64] as they are "permeable roles."[65] This is significant, for in the same section of her book she goes on to state that "those *who don't yet know the Lord* are summoned for food *and fellowship*."[66] Whereas the Scriptures state unambiguously that "if we [Christians] walk in the light, as he is in the light, *we have fellowship with one another*,"[67] and that this is due to our already having fellowship "with the Father and with his Son Jesus Christ,"[68] Butterfield states that unbelievers are to be summoned for fellowship, implying that they are capable of engaging in Christian fellowship. This concept of hospitality not only stands in contradiction to what is taught in Scripture, it also suggests that those outside of Christ may move by degrees to being in Christ, and not by an instantaneous and radical break from being children of darkness to being children of light.

This is further suggested by Butterfield's opening lines, wherein she states that "those who live [out radical hospitality] see strangers *as* neighbors and neighbors *as* family of God."[69] Logically, her words imply that strangers, indiscriminately considered, are to be engaged with as family of God.[70] This flatly contradicts the Scriptures, wherein the Holy Spirit says –

> Do not be unequally yoked with unbelievers. For what partnership has righteousness with lawlessness? Or what fellowship has light with darkness? What accord has Christ with Belial? Or what portion does a believer share with an unbeliever? What agreement has the temple of God with idols? For we are the temple of the living God; as God said,

> "I will make my dwelling among them and walk among them,
> and I will be their God,
> and they shall be my people.
> Therefore go out from their midst,
> and be separate from them, says the Lord,
> and touch no unclean thing;
> then I will welcome you,
> and I will be a father to you,
> and you shall be sons and daughters to me,
> says the Lord Almighty."[71]

Butterfield elsewhere explains that hospitality *renders* strangers *into* neighbors and neighbors *into* family of God.[72] However, this does not eliminate the problem mentioned above, for this rendering is a movement from one identity (non-Christian) to another (Christian) that is brought about through "radical ordinary hospitality," in which boundaries between guest and host are permeable, and the hosts (i.e. Christians) and guests (i.e. non-Christians) engage in "fellowship," an engagement which would effectively erase, or trivialize, the distinction between those who are in fellowship with God and with his Son (i.e. Christians) and those who are not (i.e. non-Christians).

A person's identity is, it seems, fluid, moving along a continuum that begins *outside* the covenant family of God and ends *in* the covenant family of God, with each of these respective social spheres having permeable boundaries. What makes this more troubling is that in her earlier work Butterfield explicitly states that "*all* acts of self-representation exist on a *continuum*, and a *continuum* allows for *fluidity* and *overlap*."[73] This universal "all" logically includes one's self-representation as a Christian. Indeed, Butterfield explicitly states that "if you stand in the risen Christ alone, *your self-representation is Christian.*"[74] This, therefore, necessarily implies that if one's self-representation is "on a continuum" that "allows for fluidity and overlap," then one's self-representation as a Christian is likewise one with permeable boundaries separating believer from unbeliever, child of God from child of wrath, righteous from unrighteous, living from dead.

Yet in what appears to contradict her belief that *all* acts of self-representation exist on a continuum, she writes –

> ...the Bible's categories for self-representation are binaries: you are either saved or you are lost. If you are saved, you are saved for God's glory and his

righteousness. He made the categories, and you don't get to blur the boundaries.[75]

These seemingly contradictory words are followed by Butterfield once again repeating that –

Self-representation[76] travels on a continuum, as words can describe or identify a sense of deep and abiding persistency (situated on the continua of self-representation and identity), and assert an allegiance (situated in community).[77]

How these are to be reconciled is unclear.[78] However, what is clear is that when "true" hospitality is viewed as a place where host and guest are permeable, in which the host is a Christian and the guest is a non-Christian, the lines between the Bible's categories are blurred.

Significantly, moreover, Butterfield explains her movement from being heterosexual to being homosexual in just this way. She writes –

I...preferred the company of women. In my late twenties, enhanced by feminist philosophy and LGBT political advocacy, my homosocial preference morphed into homosexuality. That shift was subtle, not startling. My lesbian identity and my love for my LGBT community developed in sync with my lesbian sexual practice. Life finally came together for me and made sense.[79]

Butterfield's movement from heterosexuality to homosexuality, in other words, happened by degrees as she was influenced by feminist philosophy and LGBT advocacy, worked within the LGBT community, and engaged in lesbian sexual activity. What is clearly portrayed is a movement from the outside (heterosexuality) to the inside (homosexuality), which is facilitated by a third both/and factor (homosociality) which allows for participation in a community's practices (LGBT political advocacy and lesbian sexual practice).

Her description of her movement into the LGBT community is eerily reminiscent of her description of her movement into the community of God's people. Between heterosexuality and homosexuality, binarily opposed sexual identities, Buttefield sets before us a bridge – *homosociality* – which is neither heterosexual nor homosexual. This idea of a both/and bridge between binaries is present throughout *TGH.* In the book, Butterfield gives emphasis to the *imago dei* as the both/and common factor between *insiders* (i.e. Christians) and *outsiders* (i.e. unbelievers) facilitating conversion from the latter to the former, and allowing for outsiders to actively engage in insider practices (e.g. psalm singing, discussing Scripture, etc).

Butterfield's continuum thinking in these later works is, moreover, reflective of her pre-Christian academic work. In *The Politics of Survivorship: Incest, Women's Literature, and Feminist Theory* Butterfield presents the same idea of transitioning from *outside* to *inside* by means of a common both/and factor, a bridge, facilitating the transition by allowing for interaction between the binary pair. Explaining why she chose to engage with novels in her book, she writes –

> If novels can...be seen as a site of historical agency, then we can see how they serve to bridge the binaries that divide our social order: inside/outside, public/private, false/true. That is, novels are always already on both sides of the binary pair.[80]

Thus, in the context of *The Politics of Survivorship* it is the novel that serves as a bridge between binaries dividing the social order. Like the postmodernists she learned from, Butterfield presents subjectivity as *fluid*, moving along a *continuum*, and facilitated by a third both/and factor that sits on both sides of a given binary pair.

4. The Feminist-Theological Ethic of Hospitality

The traces of Derridean hospitality, Levinasian theo-anthropological ethics, and postmodern fluid subjectivity are present in *TGH*. It may be difficult to see how they can simultaneously co-exist in any book, let alone within a putatively Christian book, until one recalls that postmodern philosophy encourages blurring, mixing, and even "holding in dialectical tension"[81] ideas that are utterly opposed to one another. Rather than converting to Derridean Deconstructionism or Levinasian Meta-ontologism, the postmodern thinker creates a bricolage of concepts, a mosaic of ideas that transgress lines of demarcation drawn between disciplines (e.g. literature and philosophy), and between philosophers (e.g. Jacques Derrida and Alain Badiou).

This is true of postmodernists in general, but also of feminism in particular. Maurice Hamington notes that in the field of *ethics* feminist philosophers, in part following Derrida and Levinas, have begun to argue that *"hospitality* is a glaring moral imperative because of the escalation of world violence, global disparities in quality-of-life issues, international alliances, globalization, and widespread migration."[82] Hamington further explains that –

> ...Emmanuel Levinas (1969) and Jacques Derrida (2001) have offered rich explorations of hospitality, the significance of which has not been exhausted by contemporary commentators.
>
> [...]
>
> Although Derrida and Levinas have revitalized philosophical interest in hospitality, feminist ethicists have advanced alternatives to traditional moral theory that...can coalesce and contribute to a robust understanding of hospitality—that is, identity, inclusiveness, reciprocity, forgiveness, and embodiment.
>
> At a minimum, feminist hospitality drives at a nonhierarchical understanding of hospitality that mitigates the expression of power differential, while seeking greater connection and understanding for the mutual benefit of both host and guest.
>
> [...]
>
> [This form of] hospitality...is embedded in a positive human ontology that pursues evocative exchanges to foster better understanding. In this manner, feminist

hospitality explores the antimony between disruption and connection: The guest and host disrupt each other's lives sufficiently to allow for meaningful exchanges that foster interpersonal connections of understanding. To this end...feminist hospitality reflects a performative extension of care ethics that seeks to knit together and strengthen social bonds through psychic and material sharing.[83]

Hamington is not alone in proposing this kind of feminist hospitality, finding like-minded contemporaries in feminist theology.

Kate Ward asserts that "by far the most in-depth and interesting recent work on the virtue of hospitality *comes from authors with implicit or explicit feminist commitments.*"[84] This is revealing, given that there are many points of agreement – some even using nearly identical descriptions – between these feminist theologians and Butterfield. For instance, Butterfield, who believes that for most people "hospitality conjures up a scene of a *Victorian tea*...and...paisley-patterned teacups,"[85] echoes "feminist authors [who] *universally* denounce visions of hospitality as 'cozy' and 'sentimental,' what Letty Russell associates with '*tea and crumpets*'...and 'terminal niceness.'"[86] Additionally, Butterfield declares that "radically ordinary Christian hospitality *does not happen in La La Land,*"[87] echoing the sentiment of feminist theologian "Elizabeth Newman [who] blasts '*Disney World hospitality*' which paints God's realm as a magic kingdom of ease, free from challenge."[88] Butterfield's assertion that "[hospitality]...*forces us to deal with diversity and difference of opinion,*"[89] moreover, is nearly identical to feminist theologians'

31

claims that "since hospitality by definition is practiced *across boundaries of difference*, it *forces host and guest to acknowledge and embrace their own differences* rather than attempting to erase them."[90]

Butterfield's doctrine of hospitality, moreover, puts emphasis on accepting guests *just as they are,* reflecting yet another aspect of the contemporary feminist-theological doctrine of hospitality. As Ward explains, feminist theologians argue that "hospitality...insists *on encountering the other as she is, in her particularity*, resisting any easy erasure of deeply felt distinctions of identity."[91] This come-as-you-are principle was a crucial factor in Butterfield's relationship with Ken and Floy Smith, the Christian couple through whom she became introduced to Christianity, and who are presented throughout *TGH* as exemplary models of Christian hospitality. Butterfield writes –

> Ken and Floy Smith treaded carefully with me. Early in our friendship, Ken made the distinction between acceptance and approval. He said that he accepted me just as I was but that he did not approve.[92]

For Butterfield and contemporary feminist theologians, accepting the other *just as she is* can be a risky endeavor, but that does not justify creating protective "walls" around our homes. When facing the risks involved with engaging in radical hospitality, Butterfield states that –

> One option is to build the walls higher, declare more vociferously that our homes are our castles, and, since

the world is going to hell in a handbasket, we best get inside, thank God for the moat, and draw up the bridge. Doing so practices war on this world but not the kind of spiritual warfare that drives out darkness and brings in the kindness of the gospel. Strategic wall building serves only to condemn the world and the people in it.[93]

This sentiment is identical in essence to that which is expressed by feminist theologians. For instance, Ward quotes Jessica Wrobleski who argues that

'The legitimate need for safety can become so exaggerated that it builds walls of suspicion and hostility in place of limits of hospitality [...] While a measure of security is necessary for the creation of safe and friendly spaces, making the need for security absolute can also become idolatrous.' [94]

The idolatry she mentions is related to personal possessions because hospitality comes "*at the cost of* [possible] *danger and plunder from others.*"[95] And this, too, echoes Butterfield's doctrine of hospitality in which concerns over one's personal possessions that sets up "walls" or limits to the practice of hospitality are thought to be related to idolatry. Butterfield writes –

...Christians who have too much are the ones prohibited from practicing hospitality. They have so many cluttered idols that they can give nothing at all. For this reason, it is often the well-heeled and rich who are known for their lack of hospitality, and the meager and even poor who are known for their plentiful hospitality.[96]

For Butterfield, moreover, true hospitality entails the interchangeability of guest and host roles. She writes –

> In radically ordinary hospitality, host and guest are interchangeable.
>
> [...]
>
> Radically ordinary hospitality means that hosts are not embarrassed to receive help, and guests know that their help is needed.[97]

This view is identical in substance to that of contemporary feminist theologians, as Ward explains –

> Feminist theologians insist that hospitality can describe an exchange that brings benefit to those on each side. As Wrobleski writes, 'the best experiences of hospitality are often those in which guests take on some of the roles of hosts and hosts also experience the presence of their guests as refreshment and gift'...Russell concurs: 'Hospitality is a two-way street of mutual ministry where we often exchange roles and learn the most from those whom we considered 'different' or "other."'[98]

Butterfield and the feminist theologians believe that hospitality deconstructs the rigid binary of guest and host, treating the roles as permeable, fluid, interchangeable.

5

Conclusions

In conclusion, let us review the ways in which Christian hospitality and Butterfieldian hospitality are at odds with one another, a reality which results in the subversion of Christian orthodoxy, and then conclude with an admonition to Christians to steer clear of Butterfield's writings. For instance, we note that whereas Christian hospitality maintains a strict distinction between host and guest, Butterfieldian hospitality maintains that the roles of guest and host are permeable and, therefore, aims to deconstruct the binary opposition of host and guest, thereby rendering them interchangeable. Moreover, we also note that whereas Christian hospitality is evaluative, involving the fixed roles of guest and host, and can lead to either (a.)the guest revealing himself to be an enemy, or (b.)the guest revealing himself to be a friend,[99] Butterfield's doctrine of hospitality is not evaluative but rehabilitative and transformative. Additionally, Scripture clearly and repeatedly identifies the subjects of hospitality as Christians, whereas Butterfieldian hospitality views all strangers indiscriminately as the subjects of hospitality.

We must also add that Butterfieldian hospitality seemingly flows from the assumption that subjectivity is fluid, whereas Christian hospitality does not. Thus, the former seems to allow for a social transition from outsider (i.e. non-Christian) to insider (i.e. Christian) by a gradual progression facilitated by a common third factor (i.e. the imago dei), whereas the latter clearly articulates that becoming a Christian is not a gradual process but a radical and immediate transformation accomplished by the Spirit of God.

Likewise, Butterfieldian hospitality indiscriminately assumes all people – saved or unsaved – have the potential to reflect the image of Christ, a view based in part on her misinterpretation of Matt 25:36-41. However, Christian hospitality strictly maintains that bearing the image of Christ is the end goal of sanctification and, consequently, glorification. This means that it is not the stranger or guest indiscriminately considered who can show us Jesus, but *only* Christian strangers or guests.

Finally, whereas Christian hospitality is derived from a proper exegesis of the Scriptures, Butterfieldian hospitality is derived from postmodernism, feminism, and feminist theology. Butterfield not only gives us the linguistic and conceptual data we need to draw that conclusion, she explicitly states –

> Hospitality renders our houses hospitals [i.e. places of rehabilitation] and incubators [i.e. places of growth/-transformation]. When I was in a lesbian community, this is how we thought of our homes. I learned a lot in that community about how to shore up a distinctive culture within and to live as a despised but hospitable

and compassionate outsider in a transparent and visible way. I learned how to create a habitus that reflected my values to a world that despised me.

I learned to face my fears and feed my enemies.

[...]

This idea—that our houses are hospitals and incubators—was something I learned in my lesbian community in New York in the 1990s....we set out to be the best neighbors on the block. We gathered in our people close and daily, and we said to each other, "This house, this habitus, is a hospital and an incubator. We help each other heal, and we help ideas take root."[100]

Butterfieldian hospitality is the fruit of a postmodern feminist-theological worldview that stands opposed to Christianity on the issues mentioned throughout the course of this essay.

6

Admonitions

While *The Gospel Comes With a House Key* is not devoid of explicit statements of orthodox Christian belief, those expressions of orthodoxy are not the source material from which Butterfield has derived her doctrine of hospitality. Resultantly, her writing is a mixture of postmodern-feminist-theological language and concepts, on the one hand, and Reformed Presbyterian theology, on the other hand. This, at best, is due to inconsistent thinking and terminological imprecision. At worst, Butterfield's writing is purposefully presenting a mixture of contradictory ideas for the sake of indirectly teaching readers to disregard or undermine the Scriptures' teaching on hospitality, trading it for another version of hospitality that justifies the social justice "Gospel" by identifying social justice activity as part and parcel of the "ground zero" of the Christian life, namely *radically ordinary hospitality*.

That the latter seems to be the case is based, in part, on the most charitable reading one can have of a book written by a thinker whose knowledge of postmodern and feminist philosophy prior to her conversion was anything but deficient, asystematic, or unclear. *The Politics of Survivorship*, as well as her various academic articles and book reviews,[101] demonstrate how proficiently, systematically, and clearly Butterfield is capable of writing and reading. This casts a dark shadow over *TGH*, for in it she presents contradictory data (orthodox and unorthodox beliefs, postmodern and Reformed beliefs, and so forth), purposefully misinterprets Scripture to support her doctrine of hospitality, and promotes various social justice causes that have rightly been called into question by many sound Reformed thinkers concerned with the infiltration of critical race theorists into otherwise theologically sound, Reformed churches and institutions of higher learning.

Abuse of Scripture

Above, we have examined Butterfield's misappropriation of Matthew 25:31-46 in her presentation of how Christians are failing to show hospitality to the stranger during the so-called refugee crisis. Here we must also draw attention to her eisegetical reading of Luke 24:13-17. Concerning Jesus' interaction with the disciples on the road to Emmaus, Butterfield writes –

> This passage in Luke spills over with grace and care. Jesus models here what the future of our daily, ordinary, radical hospitality is all about.

> First, Jesus does not come with an apologetics lesson. He comes with a question. And then he listens compassionately as the two share pain, disappointment,

abandonment, betrayal. The pain in their heart is extreme, so much so that they must stop walking to compose themselves. And they don't just stop—they stand still. The drama in the narrative halts with this reality: "And they stood still, looking sad."

They are going somewhere, but they don't know why. They lose their vision. A question derails them.

That happens to a lot of people.

Jesus does not hurry them. He does not jolly them. He doesn't fear their pain or even their wrong-minded notions of who the Christ should be or is.

[...]

The men tell their side of the story... [and] Jesus, after hearing their side of the story, speaks words of grace, words that tell the whole story, words that expose the goodness of both law and grace.

[...]

Jesus tells his fellow travelers that nothing has happened apart from what the Old Testament prophesied: the sufferings of the Christ are the appointed path to glory. The Old Testament had prepared them to hear this, but the cross itself became a stumbling block. Severity. Humiliation. They knew their Scriptures, but seeing them in the backdrop of the cross was too much to bear. Because it is too much to bear. And that is why Jesus takes their hands—and ours—and walks with us. Grace does not make the hard thing go away; grace illumines the hard thing with eternal meaning and purpose.[102]

Butterfield's sentimental eisegesis of this narrative fails to deal with Jesus' stern rebuke of the disciples. Luke records the following taking place within that very narrative –

And [Jesus] said to them, "O foolish ones, and slow of heart to believe all that the prophets have spoken! Was it not necessary that the Christ should suffer these things and enter into his glory?" And beginning with Moses and all the Prophets, he interpreted to them in all the Scriptures the things concerning himself.[103]

Christ's identification of these disciples as foolish and slow of heart to believe is not a compliment. Rather, it is a stern rebuke to these individuals who should have known better but, because of their unbelief, were disillusioned, sad.

Absent from the text is the idea that the disciples had to compose themselves due to the overwhelming nature of their grief. Absent from the text is the idea that these disciples *knew their Scriptures*, but were too emotionally overwhelmed to properly understand them in light of the crucifixion of Jesus. Absent from the text is the idea that Jesus took the hands of these disciples into his own because he knew their emotions were overwhelmed in light of the crucifixion. These are all read into the text in order to support Butterfield's doctrine of hospitality, as if Christ engaged in that same practice which identifies as Christian hospitality. The problem, however, is that the text neither explicitly nor implicitly teaches those things. Butterfield reads her ideas into this text in order to claim that Christ himself exemplified the doctrine she is promoting, but he did no such thing.

Social Justice

Adding to her misinterpretation of Scripture, we also can find the promotion of social justice activism under the guise of "radically ordinary hospitality" in *TGH*. For instance, Butterfield states that because the Gospel is "cosmological and holistic" [104]

> When a church identifies a sin pattern of its people (such as pornography), it also has a responsibility to protect the victims created by that sin. Repentance calls for nothing short of this. [105]

The reasoning put forward by Butterfield here is extremely problematic. For if the sin pattern of a church is replaced with, for instance, the sin pattern of "white privilege" or "class privilege," then it follows that if the church is to *truly* repent, then it must protect the victims of "white privilege" and/or "class privilege."

This inference is likely sound given that Butterfield herself believes she benefits from "class and racial privilege,"[106] and argues that

> ...Christians are coconspirators [in the evils perpet-

uated by the "post-Christian" world in which we live]....Our cold and hard hearts; our failure to love the stranger; our selfishness with our money, our time, and our home; and our privileged back turned against widows, orphans, prisoners, and refugees mean we are guilty in the face of God of withholding love and Christian witness.[107]

And when reflecting on how she addresses women in the LGBT community, showing "respect" to them by describing their relationships according to their own standards, she writes –

I ponder: Have I made myself safe to share the real hardships of your day-to-day living, or am I still so burdened by the hidden privileges of Christian acceptability that I can't even see the daggers in my hands? Am I safe? If not, then why not?[108]

"Christian privilege" is a the conceptual fruit of critical theory, as are racial, class, and heterosexual privilege – and Butterfield embraces all of them as legitimate.[109] Thus, while Butterfield contrasts "the social gospel" with "radical ordinary Christian hospitality," she still embraces the critical theory ensconced social justice concepts that she claims to have left behind years ago. Even more problematically, she believes that it is the Christian's moral duty to socially engage as if these critical theory ideas are legitimate. As she states in the opening of her book –

Those who live out radically ordinary hospitality [i.e. obedient Christians, as she elsewhere explains] see their homes not as theirs at all but as God's gift to use for the furtherance of his kingdom. They open doors; they seek out the underprivileged.[110]

If the church is to address sin patterns like racial, class, heterosexual, and Christian privilege, then the church is, by Butterfield's reasoning, is to engage in social justice (as defined by critical theorists and critical race theorists).

Butterfield's doctrine of hospitality is neither biblical nor innocuous. Rather, it subtly introduces a means whereby biblically constituted orthodox walls around the church may be slowly broken down under the guise of showing hospitality. There are contemporary theologians who, in fact, have used this feminist-theological doctrine of hospitality to promote religious inclusivism. While it may seem to be that Butterfield has important insights into LGBTQ+ issues, she is rehashing postmodernist feminist and feminist-theological concepts, none of which is compatible with Christianity. We admonish Christians, therefore, to not look to her books for guidance in how Christians are to share the Gospel with our neighbors, homosexual *or* heterosexual. Scripture is sufficient to address the matter, and it does. It is not radical ordinary hospitality that is the power of God unto salvation, but the Gospel *alone*.

Notes

INTRODUCTION

1   February 7, 2013, https://www.christianitytoday.com/ct/2013/january-february/my-train-wreck-conversion.html, Accessed December 30, 2019.

2   ibid.

3   ibid.

4   Butterfield explains that her conversion to Christianity marked her as a turncoat and traitor among her intellectual peers.

5   In the course of this essay, we will show that the postmodern ideas embedded in *The Gospel Comes With a House Key* are present throughout her writings, including her preconversion academic writing.

HOSPITALITY IS DECONSTRUCTION

6   *Acts of Religion,* Ed. Gil Anidjar (New York: Routledge, 2002), 364.

7   "Interruptions: Derrida and Hospitality," in *Kritike* Vol. 2 No. 1 (June, 2008), 4. (emphasis added)

8   "Hospitality: The Apostle John, Jacques Derrida, and Us," Third Millennium Ministries, Accessed Jan 13, 2020, https://thirdmill.org/articles/-jas_foster/jas_foster.hospitality.html.(emphasis added)

9   i.e. an irresolvable internal contradiction or logical disjunction in a text, argument, or theory.

10   *Interruptions*, 5. (emphasis added)

11   *Phenomenologies of the Stranger: Between Hostility and Hospitality,* ed. Richard Kearney and Kascha Semonovitch (New York: Fordham University Press, 2011),12.

12   *Of Hospitality: Anne Dufourmantelle Invites Jacques Derrida to Respond,* Trans. Rachel Bowlby (Stanford: Stanford University Press, 2000), 77.

13   i.e. diametrically opposed pairs (e.g. good/evil, life/death, divine/demonic)

DERRIDEAN HOSPITALITY VS. CHRISTIAN HOSPITALITY

14   *Of Hospitality,* 77. (emphasis added)

15   *Hospitality: The Apostle John, Jacques Derrida, and Us.*

16   ibid.

17   *Interruptions,* 1-2. (emphasis added)

18   "Entertaining Angels: Early Christian Hospitality in its Mediterranean Setting," Review of *Entertaining Angels: Early Christian Hospitality in its Mediterranean Setting,* in *Interpretation: A Journal of Bible and Theology* Vol. 62 (January: 2008), 102. (emphasis added)

19   *Hospitality: The Apostle John, Jacques Derrida, and Us.*

20   ibid.

BUTTERFIELD'S POSTMODERN ROOTS

21   *TGH,* (emphasis added)

22   ibid.

23   ibid.

24   ibid.

25   ibid. (emphasis added)

26   *ibid. (emphasis added)*

27   ibid. (emphasis added)

28   ibid. (emphasis added)

29   ibid. (emphasis added)

30   ibid. (emphasis added)

31   ibid. (emphasis added)

32   ibid. (emphasis added)

33   ibid. (emphasis added)

34   "Violence and Postmodernism: A Conceptual Analysis," in *Reason Papers* 32 (Fall: 2010), 67.

35   ibid. (emphasis added)

36   "Language, Violence, and Human Rights Law," in *Yale Journal of Law & the Humanities,* Vol. 11, Iss. 2 [1999], 215-216.

37   *TGH.*

38   ibid.

39 ibid. (emphasis added)

40 ibid. (emphasis added)

41 Col 3:1-11. (emphasis added)

42 See Eph 4:20-24.

43 Rom 8:28-30. (emphasis added)

44 cf. John 8:42-44; Gen 3:1 , Rev 12:9, & Matt 3:7, 12:34, 22:33, & 1st John 3:7-10.

45 See James 3:6b-10.

46 "Beyond Atheism and Atheology: The Divine Humanism of Emmanuel Levinas," in *Religions* 10:131 (2019), 3. (emphasis added)

47 "Reading Levinas on Ethical Responsibility," in *Responsibility and Commitment: Eighteen Essays in Honor of Gerhold K. Becker,* ed. Tze-wan Kwan (Edition Gorz: 2008), 156.

48 *Is It Righteous to Be? Interviews with Emmanuel Levinas,* ed. Jill Robbins (Stanford: Stanford University Press, 2001), 255. (emphasis added)

49 ibid., 52.

50 ibid., 171. (emphasis added)

51 Matt 25:40.

52 Matt 12:50.

53 cf. Matt 28:10 & 16.

54 Heb 2:11-12. (emphasis added)

55 Rom 12:13. (emphasis added)

56 1st Tim 5:9-10. (emphasis added)

57 Heb 13:1-3. (emphasis added)

58 1st Pet 4:7-10. (emphasis added)

59 *Merriam-Webster*, s.v. "Subjectivity," Accessed Jan 20, 2020, https://www.merriam-webster.com/dictionary/subjectivity.

60 *Merriam-Webster*, s.v. "Subjective," Accessed Jan 20, 2020, https://www.merriam-webster.com/dictionary/subjective.

61 "On the Problem of Subjectivity," in *Russian Studies in Philosophy*, vol. 56, no. 1, 2018, 1-2.

62 For a helpful introduction to this topic, see Hearfield, James. "Postmodernism and the Death of the Subject," Marxists.org, https://www.marxists.org/reference/subject/philosophy/works/en/heartfield-james.htm.

63 ibid., 4.

64 TGH.

65 ibid.

66 ibid. (emphasis added)

67 1st John 1:7. (emphasis added)

68 1st John 1:3.

69 *TGH*. (emphasis added)

70 The law of transitivity states – If A is B, and B is C, then A is C. Thus, Butterfield's opening line could be restated, according to the law of transitivity, as follows:

If strangers (indiscriminately considered) are to be engaged with as neighbors
  and neighbors (indiscriminately considered) are to be engaged with as family of God,
  then strangers (indiscriminately considered) are to be engaged with as family of God.

71 2nd Cor 6:14-18. (emphasis added)

72 Butterfield writes:

My prayer is that you would see that practicing daily, ordinary, radical hospitality toward the end of rendering strangers neighbors and neighbors family of God is the missing link.

[...]

This gospel call that *renders strangers into neighbors into family of God* is all pretty straight up when you read the Bible, especially the book of Acts. And *it requires both hosts and guests.* We must participate as both hosts and guests—not just one or the other—as giving and receiving are good and sacred and connect people and communities in important ways.

[...]

All these lists lead to this moment, *when strangers are rendered brothers and sisters in Christ,* heads bowed; when the Holy Spirit drives, Jesus speaks, and we receive.

TGH. (emphasis added)

73   *Openness Unhindered: Further Thoughts of an Unlikely Convert.* (emphasis added)

74   ibid. (emphasis added)

75   ibid. (emphasis added)

76   The absence of quantification or specification here implies *universality*. Butterfield is not speaking of one kind of self-representation over and against Christian self-representation, in other words, but of self-representation in general/universally.

77   *Openness Unhindered,* ibid. (emphasis added)

78   One possible solution to this contradiction can be found in Butterfield's preconversion article titled "Feminism, Essentialism, and Historical Context," in *Women's Studies* Vol.25 (1995). There she writes –

My position…is that essentialism and constructionism, as theoretical positions that determine ways of reading, *are not mutually exclusive*, but *inseparable and interdependent*; they are *complicated versions of each other*. Although the doctrinaire anti-essentialist would necessarily resist this assertion out-of-hand, what we see when filtering the essentialist-constructionist binarism through a psychoanalytic/poststructural frame is that essence (essentialism) is to counter-essence (constructionism) as transference is to counter-transference.

…Thus, essentialism is only negatively charged when it operates as a critical return of the repressed.

[96-97, emphasis added]

In other words, for Butterfield fixity and fluidity as regards subjectivity are not mutually exclusive. Rather, they are interdependent, complicated versions of each other. If Butterfield still maintains this view, then her contradicting beliefs may be capable of harmonization.

79   ibid. (emphasis added)

80   *The Politics of Survivorship: Incest, Women's Literature, and Feminist Theory,* (New York: New York University Press, 1996)4. (emphasis added)

81   i.e. *contradiction.*

82   "Toward a Theory of Feminist Hospitality," in *Feminist Formations*, Vol. 22 No. 1 (Spring), 22-23. (emphasis added)

83   ibid. (emphasis added)

84   "Jesuit and Feminist Hospitality: Pope Francis' Virtue Response to Inequality," in *Religions* 8, 71 (2017), 4. (emphasis added)

85   *TGH.*

86   *Jesuit and Feminist Hospitality*, 4.

87   *TGH.* (emphasis added)

88   *Jesuit and Feminist Hospitality*, 4. (emphasis added)

89   *TGH.*

90   *Jesuit and Feminist Hospitality*, 5. (emphasis added)

91   *Jesuit and Feminist Hospitality*, 5. (emphasis added)

92   *TGH.* (emphasis added)

93   *TGH.* (emphasis added)

94   *Jesuit and Feminist Hospitality*, 6. (emphasis added) Butterfield similarly identifies concern for personal and national safety as possibly "obdurate sin." She writes –

Who should take responsibility for this global humanitarian crisis?

Is it safe to get involved?

[...]

It is deadly to ignore biblical teaching about serving the stranger—deadly to the people who desperately need help and deadly to anyone who claims Christ as King....A more crucial question for the Bible-believing Christian is this: Is it safe to fail to get involved?

[...]

Is our lack of care for the refugee and the stranger an innocent lack of opportunity, or is it a form of willful violence? Is it a reasonable act of *self-preservation*, or is it *obdurate sin*?

TGH. (emphasis added)

95 *Jesuit and Feminist Hospitality*, 6. (emphasis added)

96 *TGH.* (emphasis added)

97 *TGH.* (emphasis added)

98 7. (emphasis added)

CONCLUSIONS

99 See our foregoing discussion of ancient Mediterranean practices of hospitality, which Christians practiced, above. Additionally, see Igor Lorencin's insightful analysis of 3rd John's comments on the practice of hospitality titled "Hospitality as a Ritual Liminal-Stage Relationship with Transformative Power: Social Dynamics of Hospitality and Patronage in the Third Epistle of John," in *Biblical Theology Bulletin* Vol. 490 No. 3 (2018), 146–155. In particular, Lorencin explains –

…Normally people are treated according to their status, but with hospitality a guest's status is not important, since in the liminal stage he is in transition to obtaining a new status as household friend.

What rights does the guest have? He is supposed to be served—the host is his servant who provides for the needs of his guest. The guest is like a king in a hospitality situation—he receives services, the best seating places, the best food and drink, as well as the best accommodation in the house. Regular social order is set aside, and the host is now a servant. Refusing the offered services would offend the host and indicate that the services were not good enough. Thus, there were certain rules of hospitality, and both parties were supposed to stay within the boundaries of their roles during a single hospitality event…

[*Hospitality as Ritual*, 149.]

100 *TGH.* (emphasis added)

ADMONITIONS

101 For example, see Champagne, Rosaria M. "Women's History and Housekeeping: Memory, Representation and Reinscription," in *Women's Studies* Vol. 20 (1992), 321-329; "The Other Women's Movement," in *The Women's Review of Books* Vol. 16 No. 3 (December: 1998),, 28-29; "Passionate Experience," in *The Women's Review of Books* Vol. 13, No. 3 (December: 1995), 14-15; "Other Women: The Writing of Class, Race and Gender, 1832-1898" [Review], in *Nineteenth-Century Contexts* Vol. 15 No.1 (1991),

88-93; and "Getting Smart: Feminist Research and Pedagogy With/in the Postmodern" [Review], in *NWSA Journal* Vol. 3, No. 3 (Autumn: 1991), 477-479.

102 *TGH.* (emphasis added)

103 Luke 24:25-27.

104 This phrasing is significant in light of the fact of Butterfield's positive association with, and varied media contributions to, Desiring God, The Gospel Coalition, and The Ethics and Liberty Commission. These organizations/ministries all promote social justice as articulated by proponents of critical theory and its various offspring (e.g. critical race theory), and seem to also connect it with a "cosmological and wholistic" "gospel." See, for instance, Graves, Rayshawn. "Nothing Less Than Justice," Desiring God, August 29, 2016, https://www.desiringgod.org/articles/ nothing-less-than-justice; Wax, Trevin. "Sheep & Goats 3: Human Need," The Gospel Coalition, February 11, 2008, https://www.thegospelcoalition. org/blogs/trevin-wax/sheep-goats-3; and Hough, Casey B. "What Sheep and Goats Teach Us About the Sanctity of Life: Matthew 25 and the Least of These," Ethics and Religious Liberty Commission, January 29, 2020, https://erlc.com/resource-library/articles/what-sheep-and-goats-teach-us-about-the-sanctity-of-life.

105 *TGH.* (emphasis added)

106 ibid.

107 ibid. (emphasis added)

108 ibid. (emphasis added)

109 We have above mentioned racial and class privilege, but can add more examples here. For instance, when speaking about "Lisa"'s difficult time in medical school, Butterfield writes –

During medical school [Lisa] struggled with sleep deprivation and im- poster identity, as she was daily surrounded by people in her medical program who came with *social privilege*.
[emphasis added]

Similarly, when speaking about why some professing Christians become progressive in regards to homosexuality Butterfield writes –

They [i.e. progressive "Christians"] wish to be an ally. They desire to stand

in the gap for their friends. They want their friends to have *the same rights and privileges as they do*.
[emphasis added]

110 *TGH.* (emphasis added)

About the Author

Hiram R. Diaz III is a Reformed Baptist lay-apologist & occasional preacher. Hiram's main focus is on apologetics & scholarly writing, including philosophical and theological writing, with a lesser focus on literary theory and criticism.

He is the owner of Invospec.org, a personal blog about a multitude of issues approached from a Christian worldview. He also contributes to ThornCrownMinistries.com, and is a contributor to, and webmaster for, BiblicalTrinitarian.com, a scholarly apologetics site for which Michael R. Burgos Jr. also contributes.

Hiram's aim is to glorify God by means of the written word, effectively refuting false belief systems and leading others to faith in Jesus Christ the Son of the Living God.

You can connect with me on:

- http://invospec.org
- http://twitter.com/InvolutedGenes
- http://facebook.com/BTrinitarian
- http://thorncrownministries.com

Made in the USA
Columbia, SC
02 January 2025

51089193R00038